Small Breath

Poetry of Seasons

Mandy Whyman

Lavender Button Books

The right of Mandy Whyman to be identified as author of this work has been asserted in accordance with the Copyright, Designs and Patents Act 1988

Copyright © 2024 Mandy Whyman

All rights reserved. This book or any portion thereof may not be reproduced or used in any manner whatsoever without the express written permission of the author.

Cover image: Fabrice Villard (Unsplash)

To my Uncle Brian

who slipped away into the land

24/02/2024

greatly loved and missed

<u>24/02/2024</u>

With the news new and heavy, I look for you –

Take to the fields, to the evening

In this hemisphere that tilts towards the light,

When yours tilts away.

The trees along the line are stark-cut as hours

Black branched on the bright of a setting sky, they bite –

In the fading light, the hills beckon,

Out of reach, too far to walk

And a cloud bursts grey between here and there

Trails blown like falling smoke, falling hair, falling,

Until the evening dips all gold and tears,

With scattered clouds that skud and weep.

A haze of rain shushes low across new crops,

Letting loose the smell of soil, of memories.

Slowing, stilling, until,

Beacon-bright behind the trees

An improbable yellow moon rises, round and huge

Above the weight of houses and dimming land

And strikes a heart to wonder.

Turn to home, take the tree-lined darkened lane -

And an owl calls. Twice. Again.

Low and soft as breath -

The night breaks quiet across the fields,

The miles, the seas, the hemispheres,

Unties this grief to spool

A glimpse across continents and years

To see your straight-backed striding

Away along a dusty highveld track,

Away into the land, one hand lifted.

Not goodbye.

Go well.

"I love not Man the less, but Nature more."

Lord Byron

"The poetry of earth is never dead."

John Keats

Contents

Small Breath	13
Moth Rain	14
Thistledown	16
Evening	17
September	18
Slipping to Sleeping	19
Morning Mist	20
The Last of the Tomatoes	21
Away	22
Nights Draw In	23
Traffic	24
Moon	26
Mowing	27
A New Path	28
Lurking October	30
The Mist Lifts	31

Witch Moon	32
A Time of Parting	34
Leaves Fall	35
Planting Bulbs	36
November	37
After the Storm	38
Adrift	39
Snapshot	40
Birds like Kites	41
These Ancient Trees	42
Ice Moon	43
Hard Frost	44
Fog Bound	46
Low Sky	47
Wintered Trees	48
Rain Again	50

Small Things	52
Copper Dawn	54
Winter Solstice	55
Corn Shards	56
Stars	57
Night Fog	58
Icon	60
Blushing	62
Felling	63
Signs	64
Lanes	65
Turning	66
First Flowerings	67
Heron II	68
Elegy	70

Small Breath

Our Summers are so small

Against the seasons of the Earth

The ebb and flow of ice,

The shifting of the plates,

The reach and fall of ancient trees,

The billion turnings around the sun –

This flow of light and dark and change.

We spark, brief, against the light,

Gasp at the wonder of it all,

Search to name and tame,

Transient as mayflies,

Stake our existence in tombstones and trash –

And yet are nothing against the awe of it all.

We are the small breath,

The gasp between the acts.

All the wonderous world is beautiful without us.

Beyond us. Despite us.

Moth Rain

It rains like mist –
Moth wings of wet
Soft to the air,
To the yielding soil
And shushing wheat.

Swallows swoop breathless,
Roll and dive,
Flickering out a code
In dots and dashes
Against the rain
That falls like moth wings –
Soft

Like fabric woven –
Rain and wheat and swallows –
Eternity plucks at my skin,

Blurs the now,

Melts it all away

Into rain,

That falls soft, soft,

As moth wings.

Thistledown

High Summer

And the air of evening heat

Is filled with thistledown.

That coats the lawn

With cast off wishes

Like dandelion ghosts.

Silvered hair catches

In the rose bushes

And on the cusps of leaves:

Silken cobwebs, fairy tresses, dreams…

Diaphanous skeletons of the summer

That slips so quickly

Away.

Evening

Evening closes in
To the sound of rooks
Cawing good night
In the high sky layered in grey
And gold and white.
Midges haze lazy above the pond;
A languid breeze frays
At the edges of the heated day.

Agreeable in the comfort of chimney pots
Jackdaws `tuc-tuc' sleepy conversation,
The last winging a way darkening home.
Silence settles like a blanket,
A balm.
High above: an arrow-head,
Solitary against the rim of sky.
A single swallow
Turns and dives.

September

September eases in

Like an old friend:

All languid limbs grown long

And hair goldened with barley, wheat –

Appled cheeks reddened,

Content, glowing, ripe with harvest

And rich with sated soil.

Honeyed nostalgia

Drips from her lips

And hangs on her hem –

Trails her liquid-lit footsteps

In early mists

And late dews

As she slips, slips away,

Leaving behind

The soft smell of straw.

Slipping to sleeping

September still,

But Autumn creeps on slippered feet

To draw down the evening's skirts

And lick green edges to yellow, red;

Kneeds the ground in acorns and conkers…

She breathes cool the edges of the day,

Gathers in the sun,

Lures bright Summer down darkening lanes

Into mists and mellowness;

Kisses the ripened year

To sleeping.

Morning Mist

Morning clouds hang grey-dreaming low;
Breathe mist like gauze
Across the sleeping fields.
Trees become ghosts,
Reshaped and shifting
And copses hang like islands marooned
In a hazy sea,
Soft-edged and shrouded.

All is changed; reality altered
In downy air that muffles the world.
The road is shrunk to whitened walls;
Landmarks are made magic:
Shadows and balloons.

The Last of the Tomatoes

It is the last of the tomatoes.

The small suns roll sparse

Into the collecting bowl.

The ones that won't ripen,

Cling fast

As if they might will sun and summer

To last – just a small while longer.

Green, they grip the withering stems

As shallow roots are cleared:

Seasons end

And possibilities curtailed.

An end of dreaming.

The soil is dug, raked, covered.

Another season

Another gathering of summer's fruit

Now done.

Away

Above the tufted meadows

Swallows trace figures of eight,

Shape S-bends in the mottled sky,

Turn away from what was and now is not.

They blot the lines in morse code:

Dots and dash.

Punctuate:

Comma, colon, ellipsis.

Arrow tails sketch the map:

A way, away –

Leading Summer South,

Untying September

Until it frays into rising winds,

Flutters, flits

The way, away.

Nights Draw In

The nights draw in,

Hang candle wax on the edge of memories:

Another, another -

Darkened velvet, breathed into Winter rain.

Summer seems fleeting,

A dream against the drag of days

That stumble into dark,

Each ticking clock

Closing, closing

Until the light is lost:

Darkened velvet and the Winter rain.

Traffic

Stuck in traffic –

Tin cans on pause

While ether people

Chatter in studio cheeriness –

A soundtrack to the waiting.

Clouds skud above,

Race to the beat of a singing wind,

Drive lashing skirts of rain

That whip the trees to dervish dance.

Leaves scatter like confetti against the breaklights.

The car is buffeted,

The wind rolls over steel and glass.

Gnaws edges; whistles.

Sealed, I sit

And life whirls wild outside.

The traffic moves,

Stutters into going –

A snake of tinny otherness.

The wind and clouds and trees and all

Flow on. Unimpressed. Impervious.

Wild.

Moon

The moon!

The moon, the moon, the moon:

And clouds open curtain-up

- The moon!

As if God has punched a perfect hole

In the canvas of the sky;

A porthole of hope and wonder

As if all the rains are sunk away

With no more storms to come.

The moon.

Silver-lit and dream-cast clear,

Pulling seas and mountains,

Ships across the oceans

And small hopes and hearts

Through open windows

To soar wish-skywards

Above the darkened chimney pots.

Mowing

It will rain tomorrow,

So I mow into the September evening,

Eking green lines

Into the Summer that slips away,

Gathered in green clippings,

In the last of the sun

That reddens the crab apples

And kisses soft the cooling garden,

That breathes and turns

To the hum of mowing

Late on a September evening.

A New Path

Today

I took a new path –

Followed the sketchy directions of a fellow walker –

Beside a high bastion wall, down a narrow lane,

Climbed a wooden stile -

To where the path ran mud- thin and wood-close.

Into the heart-quickening isolation, the joy of solitude.

I let the narrow way close about me,

Gather me between nettled edges, hedges, woods.

Where the wind played out in skurries,

Exhaled away the troubles of the day

Into hollow claps of pigeon wings

And chattering of Autumned leaves

Dry beneath a gathering sky.

Then

Like a reward:

The sun broke sudden cover

And high hedges gave way to emerald green

Wide fields dotted with sleepy sheep

And chicory bright as gems.

Today

I walked where I have never walked before –

To where the land opened like an envelope,

Spooled out its many wonders,

Urged me on

With wind and woods and fields and birds,

With the heart-compass pull

Of a new path.

Lurking October

October lurks like a weight:
A shadow in a corner
And all of Summer's memories
Cannot keep it at bay.

It breathes out a heaviness,
Lets loose strands of damp and dank,
Catches all in a coat of mist and grey.
It coughs the skudding sky;
Rains the world to bleak.
Weighted,
It drums on rooftops,
Insistent and unstoppable:
"I come, I come, I come."

The clapper of a bell,
The flood that will not stop,
October lurks.

The Mist Lifts

Afternoon

And the mist lifts at last

To wake the world in dazzled bright

Of Autumned limbs that reach,

Goldened in the sudden blue of sky.

Along the edges of sodden startled fields

The wind teases boas of red and gold,

Shimmied into wakefulness.

Like a shroud lifted,

Every corner of this late-sun earth

Shines burnished bright,

And joy leaps, untethered and free

Into this memory of the day.

Witch Moon

Clouds skud the moon-ringed night –

Witches' hair

Blown grey and wild

In high gusts, storm-bound.

The wind rushes corners,

Leaps in blasts and rattles trees

In banshees' breath like olden times…

Here, in this urban row,.

Jackdaws hunker down,

Silent in chimney pot bunkers

And the street cat slinks dark and low.

The smell of rain skutters.

Gutters rattle nervous readiness.

The wind plays at vagabond:

Tumbles reckless

Over these hundred-year houses

With fingers nimble and knowing…

Above, a sky of clouds curdles,

Lit cold by a witches' moon

Storm-bound.

A Time of Parting

And now is the time of parting –
Leaves like love notes of a younger year
Dropped and discarded,
Whipped away by jealous Northern winds
Grown cold,
To flutter, fade and be forgotten -
Papered sentiments of yellowed gold.
Bud and blossom grow hard –
Become the fruits with wooden hearts
And trees are stripped and stark
While rosehips and haws hang red
Like clots.
Like kisses.
The last of Summer's blood.

Leaves Fall

Then oak leaves fall

Like butterflies

To rest on upturned fields

Where the bones of Summer's crop

Scatter pale and wear away.

The wind tugs at heartstrings,

Russet leaves like wings

That catch and carousel

And fall in faded promises;

In yearning,

For seasons lost and done.

Planting bulbs

A strange ritual:

This Autumnal digging of squirrel holes

And offerings

Of woody bulbs and corms

To the cooling earth.

Buried in small graves -

It is an act of faith –

This planting out of lifeless things

This giving into Trust:

That there will be a wakening.

That there will be a Spring.

November

November's eyes are yellow tigered,

Full of fire and bite and surge

To pluck leaves like feathers

From faltering wind-lashed trees,

And fling them by gleeful handful –

Confetti spark bright –

Scattered and whirling across the road

To pelt at cars like papered hailstones.

That bank and drift,

Embered and glowing and dying:

Fuel against the onslaught of December.

After the storm

After the storm and the new November sky
Is blank and blue and silent.
The way through the woods is zebra-striped
In gold and ghosts
Of leaves, scattered like hearts:
A rug, a runner, a sometimes red carpet,
Remains of where the wind rushed
And wrenched and tore…

Gone silent now -
Red beneath the trembling sun and sleeping sky.
Bruised and blushed
After the storm.

Adrift

We drive from clear skies, descend into mist –

Cast adrift in a sea of white

Where red taillights become echoes

Of others – bearing onwards.

Trucks, wide sided, like whales

Emerge, pale-eyed and looming

To buffet at our edges

And fade away to nothing –

Swallowed by the grey shifting

Of a sea, a sea,

Where hedges drift like ghosts

And stripped trees float stark as rigging.

And reality becomes becalmed…

And then

The rise - and white lines run linear clear.

The mist laps, recedes, rolls like a secret,

A thought

A memory caught in the rearview mirror.

Snapshot

This urge to capture the moment,

To glue it to eternity,

Seal it in a bell jar

So that it resonates like crystal – clear

Beyond the timings of my year.

That it remains time-stopped:

This perfect moment

When crows erupt like scattered leaves

Wind-drawn against the sky

That falls wide in November blue

And the high dancing Autumned trees

That shimmer red and yellow hues

Stung to gleaming

In the dazzled bright

Of a low-sky sun.

This snapshot. This perfection.

This moment.

Birds like Kites

Another storm blows in

On birds like kites and leaves and bullets

Scattered and strung against a skudding sky.

Crows fracture, tumble like leaves

To roll and dive and stall

While heavy-bodied pheasants

All regaled for hunting season,

Labour low across the roads

Like long tailed torpedoes.

Pigeons falter, blow backwards

And high, high

Built for storm and surge

Gulls, white-bellied and long-winged,

Slide and surf the lip,

Skilled as glider pilots

Against the coiling, broiling wind

That turns us lesser things

Inwards, to shelter.

These Ancient Trees

These trunks of ancient trees
Barked into rivers, mountains, ravines
In a slow moving of time
That we can scarce comprehend.
The silent building of layers;
Years seasoned out in rings
Of plenty and not enough,
In silences and scuttlings of small things
And this world that turns, turns…
So it is that we seem nothing –
Small and fragile skinned,
Blinked away in all our wrath and splutter,
Forgotten and outgrown in the slow upward
Reach of ancient trees.

Ice Moon

Cooling breath licks beneath doors,

Shakes windowpanes with phantom fingers…

There's a cold moon out tonight,

Sharp-edged, as Autumn turns to ice,

White in a pearlescent sky

Blown clear – like bones.

In the morning there will be a frost –

Scattered glass on grass and edges –

Dropped reflecting shards

Of a moon grown brittle; hard.

Hard Frost

Hard frost:
The fields are struck to gleaming
With sheep, long-shadowed, leaning
Under a lowing, glowing sun
That breathes the world to fantasy:
Where every twig and leaf and blade
Is spiked in a carapace of ice
And trees, so newly stripped,
Are bladed in an armoury of light.
The world is steel and silver,
Moss made mink and grass sharded,
Tar is ribboned in bright.
The air bites.

The spell slips away with the sun,
Returning a familiar world.
Only dips and bends and pond edges
Stay suspended,

Caught in the glitter, the mesmer,

The passing ice dream

Of hard frost.

Fog-bound

I wake to an early morning moon

Shrouded in a gauzed sky

And watch the fog trails –

Like hair and eels –

Flow up from the lows

And seep into the edges

Like memories; grow

Until washing like a wave against morning,

Dropping a curtain of whitened walls

Along the boundaries of a diminished world.

The sun becomes the moon –

A pale-eyed lantern adrift in a sea

Of dripping, clinging damp.

Fog-bound.

Silent.

Low Sky

The morning seems to hush

Where the cloud brushes the earth

And the glow of a hidden sunrise

Touches the world with blushing.

The low sky, the softened land,

The rain as fine as mist.

A morning of blurred boundaries

Where I cannot tell

Whether the day is sleeping;

Or weeping.

Wintered Trees

Ink blots stretched, sketched

Bleeding into the wash of the paper sky

Like fingers; tendrils; swords –

Reaching upwards into winter,

Gaunt, now stripped and beautiful.

These pillars, stays

Holding fast the vaulted sky

With trembling arms that have touched the years,

Breathed the seasons.

Leaf veneer worn thin by Northern winds,

Bones bared in twists and striving

And a great reaching: up, up.

These wondrous things,

These gods, earth-bound

Rooted in soil and sky.

These bridges of life and season.

These wintered trees.

Rain Again

It has rained again
And the drainage ditch
Gurgles murky with urban sediment:
Remembers when it was a stream – and free.
Now it bobs lost plastic footballs,
Licks close to the tarmacked path
So that dog walkers stop and watch
Before it plunges sewar-wards
In a rush of forgotten falls.

The sky banks into its own land
Where mountain peaks glint white
Under a distant unseen sun,
And ragged banners race
Greyed and wild as horses
Lashed to frenzy by the rousing wind
That stirs the last of the leaves

And stings the air

To weeping.

Small things

The low white winter sun

Tops the trees that edge the field,

Etches out their leafless limbs.

The path squelches mud and memories

And last season's thistle heads

Droop, steeled and sodden

As the failed weaponry

Of some rusted battle.

The glow of Autumn is December greyed.

And then:

An unexpected dance of midges

That bob like flaked glitter

To the touch of the scant sun.

Small and silly things

Lured to life by the sudden mild;

Tasting Spring far too soon

In a glimmer of hidden wishes.

They are magicked from pest to stardust –

A sudden choreography of light

Caught, momentarily

Bright against the low-sun bleak

Of this winter's field.

Copper Dawn

The morning breaks in copper –

Burnished and brittle –

Trees cut like lino print,

Sharp-edged on a porcelain sky.

Sullen fields, mud-ridged in gloom

Blink back the yellowed dawn

From puddled pools –

Shards of copper -

Brittle.

Winter Solstice

Here it is: this longest night-

Where dark and dread and dead things are-

Webbed in the spin away from sun,

Our axis tilted into dreaming.

Here it is: this longest night,

Where our frail souls are most alone

And we huddle close,

Stoke fires to stay the fear,

Bear out the long dark hours -

Cave walls and crofts and suburban boxes-

A ritual of survival, of hope,

Holding out for the long dawn

Which will break, at last,

Minutely sooner, infinitely brighter,

Tilting breath, once more, towards the sun

As low kindling of hope and life

Turns away from the longest night,

Into light.

Corn Shards

Under an unexpected sun
Shards of shorn corn, like spears,
Upright in rows, that glimmer place
In paralleled undulations of the field.
Bright.
Candles perhaps, against the dark of soil,
Dark of cloud.
Strange and something timeless:
A cog turning the seasons,
Stretching away in sinewed lines –
Sparked nerves of a sleeping earth:
Memories and promises
And bones.

Stars

The stars steel clear tonight,

Sharp in the wintered sky

Stretched taught like satin behind the sickled moon.

All ice and white –

Spangled flickerings of dreams and memories,

Of worlds beyond imagining.

In the morning there will be a frost –

Frozen light on every blade

And fields glittered to otherness -

Like magic. In the eggshell dark,

The cold of far-off constellations

Will shard this distant earth,

Drop a dust of ice through space and time,

To cast the world in stars.

Night Fog

There was a forecast for fog –
And when I wake in the night,
It is there:
Rising up between the houses
Like breath.
The street lamp is haloed, cloth-muted
The light become small and uncertain -
Ghosts and memories and dreams.
The dark becomes an other place:
Chimney pots smoked indistinct
And house edges rubbed soft,
Blurred into vapour.
Fog like a river, a porous flood
Of another time,
Flows in, as if the ancient marshes
Still hold sway.
Fence posts become reeds
And the narrow tarmacked road,

Fog-filled

Imagines in silent slipping

Of forgotten mud.

Icon

Rising like Renaissance art –
All glow and blood in faith:
The sun bursts bright an open heart
Low punched in the January dawn.
Flay-ribbed clouds strike blood-pink,
Stark-edged trees and hills lick fire.
Cold sheep stand watch in sodden fields,
Wishing, waiting:
The bright, the bright!

It cannot last.
Oranged sky banners low against the horizon,
Battle-weary gasping.
The sun, too soon smalled to burnished shield
Slips upwards,
Dripping colour into the overcast
Until it is overcome.

January draws down the curtains.

Greys the sky. Wins.

Blushing

It is the evening,

Come winter-early,

Where the low-slung languid sun

Rolls out light in unexpected loveliness

To lap the land – a blessing,

So that hedgerows burnish, blush

And weary trees, brown and sodden

Gild with sudden warmth.

Copper plays the topmost branches,

'Come weathervanes and steeples.

The fields are pastel softened.

The last of the clouds glow pink-edged.

The cold world breathes slow.

Blushes.

Felling

They fell surreptitiously –

Lights into the dusk and low winter dark.

They fell from the inside out –

Like a parasite.

Piles of wood and trucks, trucks

Working secretly, surreptitiously,

The wood is felled,

Will become a field, no doubt,

A field that floods, no doubt,

Lost to the anchorings of these stoic trees

That are felled; fall

Silently into dusk.

Signs

This commute between the first months

When the naked-limbed trees

Flash like barcodes in the passing,

Backlit by a tepid sun.

The long way-edging wall, greyed with winter

And the road that sweeps away

In ribboned dirt-flecked black.

The scent of Spring seems spooled so far away…

Then the pause, the stop:

Small time to watch,

To see the tender tremble of green

And the cautious froth of pink cherry

Flowering too soon

In the shelter of bare-limbed trees

That barcode the wakening sky.

Lanes

I take the lanes –

Meander between high hedgerows

Where the way curves and dips

Like a river -

Long cut by carts and carriages

In a path of least resistance,

Skirting forgotten copses

And waterways since dried and drained,

Diverted, so that lanes

Wander serpentine, narrow

Mud-edged and dreaming:

Maps of other times.

Turning

The Earth tilts

And suddenly we are tumbling

Back towards the Spring

Where morning leans in early light

To a robin's song. Vivid. Crystal. Clear.

My long shadow flows fluid,

Trickles across the bright

Of a field new-growth greened

Beneath an unexpected February sky:

Clear. Blue. Wide

With turning in the sharp air

Filled with a scent of promise.

First Flowerings

It's cherry-plum

That froths quite suddenly on road edges –

Like confetti in a churchyard,

White against the grey.

Indeed, there's something biblical to it all:

This fragility in profusion,

Like the cracking of the dawn

When light steals despite the dark,

When birds sing despite the rain.

The blossom blooms pale on leafless limbs,

Opens wide the tender white

Like arms and hearts that trust

That love and Spring will come.

Heron II

Gangly and straggly. Wary.

The heron is back.

Son-of-Heron, perhaps

Since no heron has visited the long Winter since

And I feared him killed,

Perhaps by some irked koi-keeper,

Or driven away to safer places

Now that the mere has been spoiled and silted –

Run-off from the building site.

Now, the heron is back:

Ankle deep in this pond, upright and watchful,

Eying fish become complacent

After the long absence…

I clap, shoo him half-heartedly away:

Glad to see him back,

Reluctant to have him stay…

Those wide wings spread,

Lift the long-legged , white-bellied bird

In slow motion. High.

I find that I am pleased –

Relieved, as if some part was missing

From the puzzle of it all.

Some link, some purpose has been restored,

Now that the heron is back.

Elegy

Over the bridge and down to the church,

The winter sun setting over the last of the fields -

These fields which are the last, here

They will build the cardboard houses to fill up quotas;

The last of the fields where wheat runs yellow

And frost collects in dips,

Where hay is stacked

And rabbits hide in hedgerows.

They will dig and build.

No matter.

The roads that ring this once-village

Have stopped the deer and killed the foxes,

So that just the small and stubborn survive

On the last of the fields.

No matter.

This wintered sun sets early –

Blushes the horizon and sketches the treed edges

Of these final fields.

The light runs in ripples,

Glancing the ridges where ploughing ran –

A river of the seasons:

Sunlight on soil.

The same sun gilds the tiles, the steeple

Of the small once-village church.

Falls in blessings like watered promises –

Paper politics thin.

They will brick and tar those fields.

No Matter.

That season, in all its ugliness, will also pass.

We are so small in the turnings of the earth,

The sun will lap the land,

Catch the crooks and crowns of trees,

Call green the silent soil.

Long after the church is gone.

About the Author:

Mandy is a poet and novelist based in Shropshire, England, where she lives with her husband, youngest daughter and an indefatigable terrier named Skipper.

Her favourite things are books, plants, trees, wild things - and tea.

This is her sixth collection of poetry.

Other works:

<u>Poetry</u>

Whispers from Southern Lands (2019)

Evidence (2019)

Fieldsong (2020)

Crow Dancing (2022)

Greening (2023)

<u>Novel</u> (MJ Whyman)

Like Water (2022)

www.ingramcontent.com/pod-product-compliance
Lightning Source LLC
Chambersburg PA
CBHW072135070526
44585CB00016B/1692